Make Your Own LED Flashlight

Julia Garstecki and
Stephanie Derkovitz

BLACK RABBIT BOOKS

Hi Jinx is published by Black Rabbit Books
P.O. Box 3263, Mankato, Minnesota, 56002.
www.blackrabbitbooks.com

Marysa Storm, editor; Michael Sellner, designer;
Omay Ayres, photo researcher

Names: Garstecki, Julia, author. | Derkovitz, Stephanie, author.
Title: Make your own LED flashlight / by Julia Garstecki and Stephanie Derkovitz.
Description: Mankato, Minnesota : Bolt/Black Rabbit Books, [2020] | Series: Hi jinx. Make your own fun | Includes bibliographical references and index. | Audience: Ages 9-12. | Audience: Grades 4 to 6.
Identifiers: LCCN 2018033590 (print) | LCCN 2018036490 (ebook) | ISBN 9781680729405 (e-book) | ISBN 9781680729344 (library binding) | ISBN 9781644660652 (paperback)
Subjects: LCSH: Flashlights–Design and construction–Juvenile literature. |Light emitting diodes–Juvenile literature.
Classification: LCC TK4388 (ebook) | LCC TK4388 .G37 2020 (print) | DDC 621.32-dc23
LC record available at https://lccn.loc.gov/2018033590

Printed in China. 1/19

Image Credits

Alamy: David J. Green - electrical, 7 (alum. tape); toons4biz, Cover (bolts), 2–3 (bolts), 4 (bolts); Black Rabbit Books: Michael Sellner, 7 (battery, light), 8 (steps), 10–11 (tools), 12–13, 13 (tools), 14, 15 (tool), 16, 18–19 (tool); Shutterstock: Arcady, 7 (sticky note); belka_35, 7 (scissors); Coprid, 7 (clear tape); Fedorov Oleksiy, 7 (pencil); Galyna G, 15 (bkgd); Georgii Red, Cover (middle bolt); Jumnong, 7 (electrical tape); Memo Angeles, Cover (bulbs), 4 (bulb), 5 (bulb), 6 (bulb), 15 (bulbs), 18 (hand), 19 (bulb), 20 (bulb), 21 (bulb); mohinimurti, Back Cover (bkgd), 4 (bkgd), 12 (bkgd); Mumut, 19 (glasses); opicobello, 10 (tear), 14 (tear); Pand P Studio, 1; Pasko Maksim, Back Cover (tear), 13 (tear), 18 (tear), 23 (tear), 24; Patoman Color, Cover (tube), 4 (tube), 23 (tube); pitju, 6 (curl), 21 (curl); Ron Dale, 5 (marker stroke), 6 (marker stroke), 14 (marker stroke), 17 (marker stroke), 18 (marker stroke), 20 (marker stroke); supawat bursuk, 7 (tp roll); tawatchai.m, Cover (limbs), 4 (limbs), 23 (limbs); totallypic, 8 (arrow, circles), 10 (arrows), 11 (arrows), 12–13 (arrows), 18 (arrow), 19 (arrow); Vector Tradition, Cover (expression), 4 (expression), 23 (expression); yavi, 20 (dance) Every effort has been made to contact copyright holders for material reproduced in this book. Any omissions will be rectified in subsequent printings if notice is given to the publisher.

Contents

Chapter 1

Get Ready for Some Fun!

Making your own fun isn't complicated. In fact, it can even be useful. Today's handy fun is a flashlight! You never know when you might need one. They're **essential** for nighttime adventures. You need one if the power goes out on a stormy night too. So get building! There's fun to be had.

Chapter 2

Let's Make It!

Building a flashlight might seem hard. But it really isn't. Just gather some supplies, and get to work. Don't worry if something doesn't work right away. Experiment until it does. And, most importantly, remember to have fun!

What You'll Need

5 mm LED light bulb with wires (with ½ inch [1 centimeter] of wire **exposed**)

toilet paper tube

1 1 x 1-inch (2.5 x 2.5-cm) piece of aluminum tape

clear tape

3-volt coin cell battery with wires (with ½ inch [1 cm] of wire exposed)

sharpened pencil

electrical tape

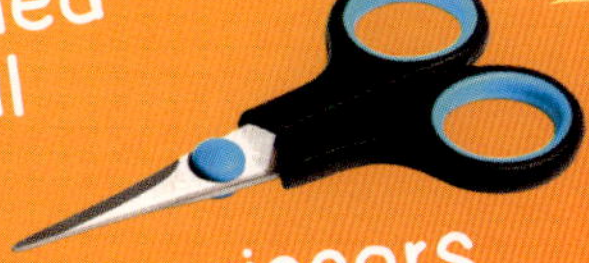

scissors

a **responsible** adult to help you

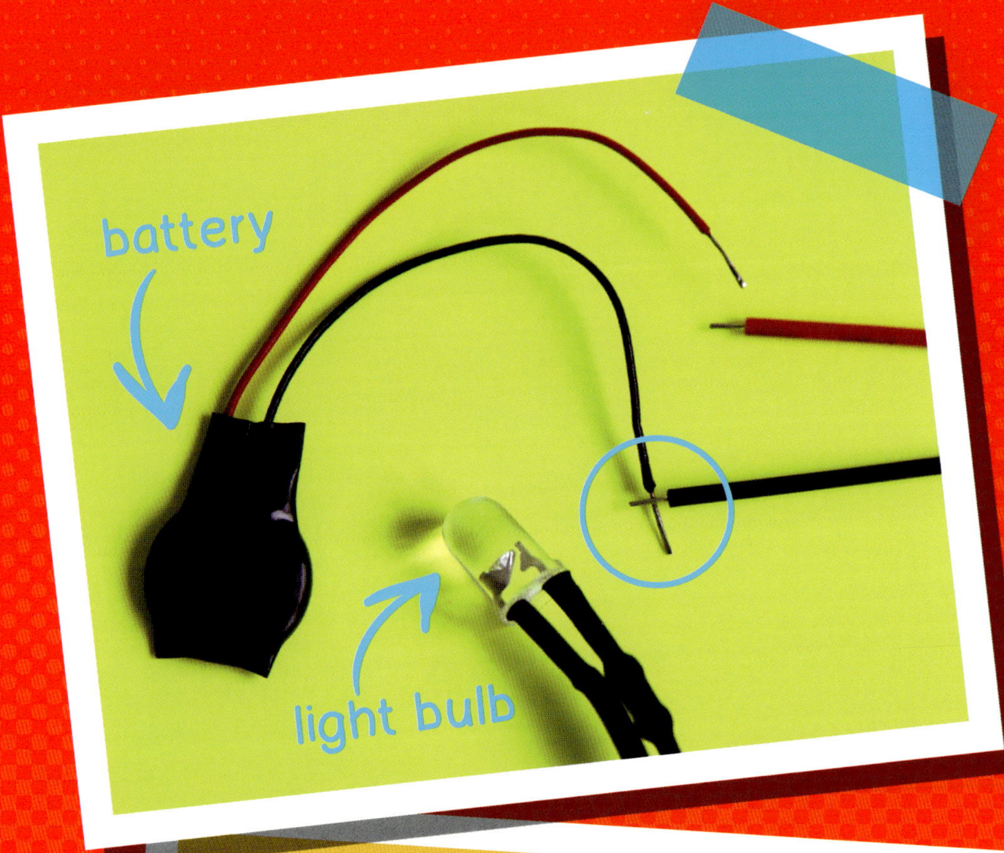
battery
light bulb

Test the Bulb and Battery

1. Touch the light bulb's black wire to the battery's black wire.

2. While keeping the black wires together, touch the red wires together. When the wires connect, the light should glow.

3. Once you've tested the light and battery, you can stop holding the wires together.

Build the Flashlight

1 Cut the toilet paper tube in half lengthwise. Set aside one half of the tube. You'll use it later.

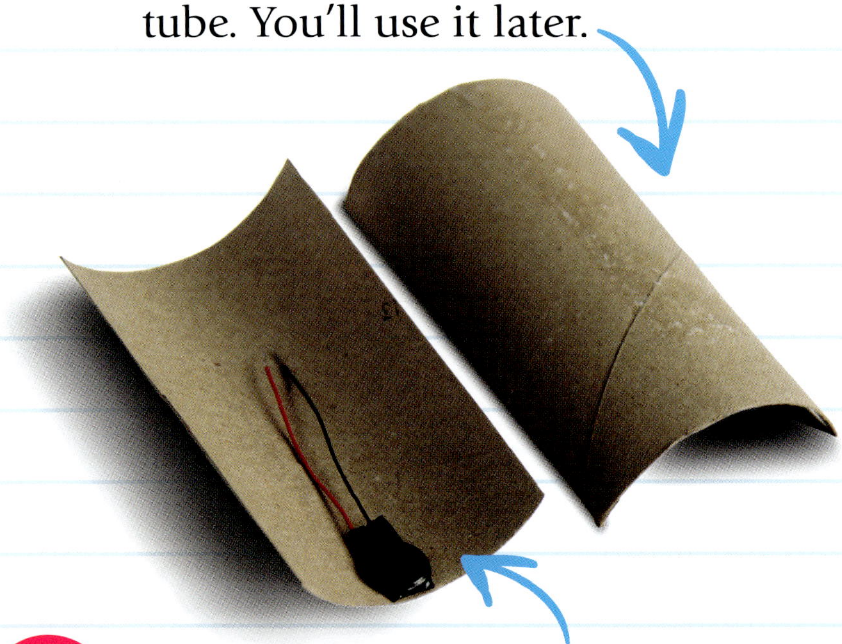

2 Place the battery on the inside of the tube. Put the battery along the bottom, and center it. There should be equal amounts of tube on either side.

3 Tape the battery down with clear tape. Keep the wires free.

4 Arrange the wires so the black wire goes up the tube. The red wire should go out the tube's bottom.

5 Place the light on the opposite side of the tube. It should be balanced on the tube's edge and across from the battery.

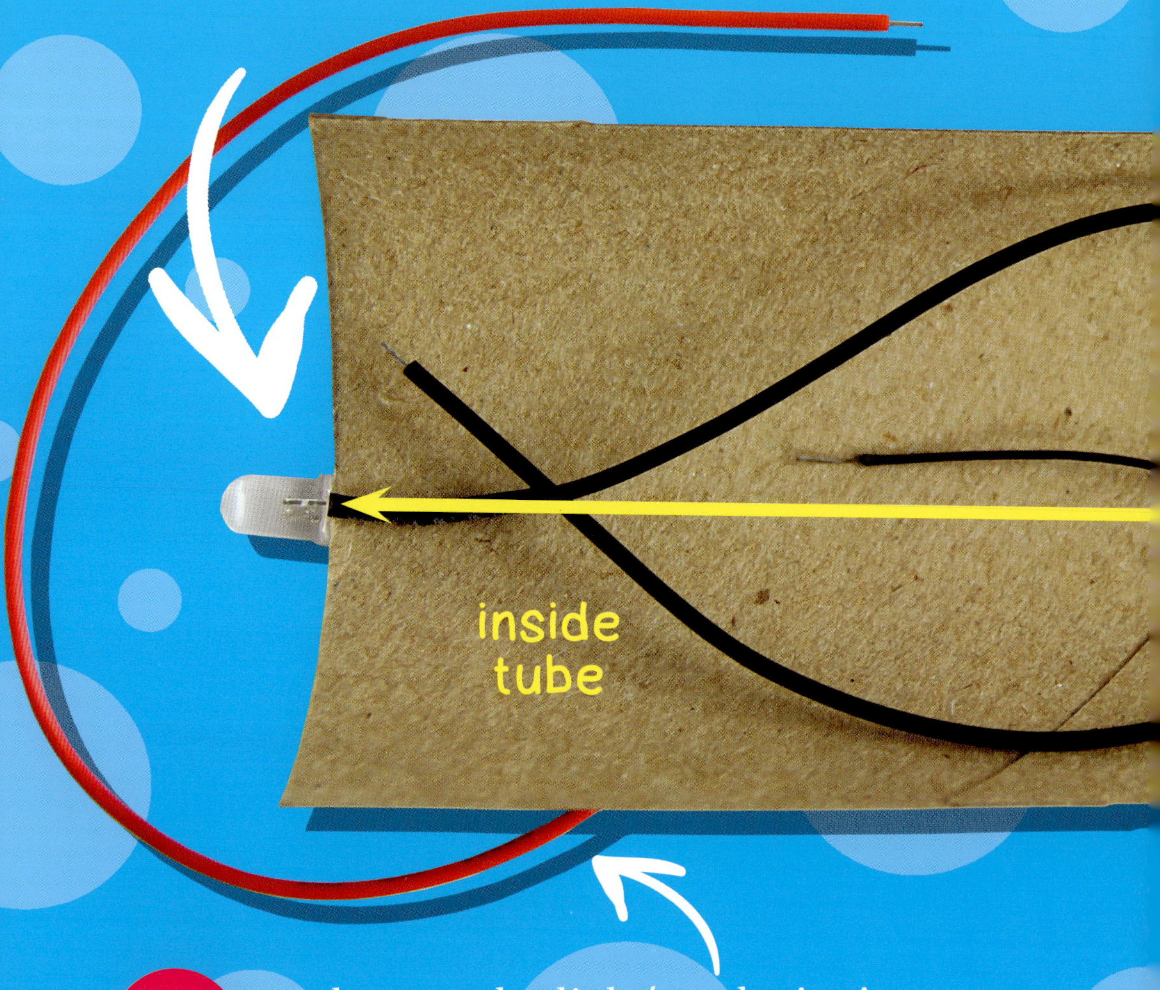

6 Make sure the light's red wire is outside of the tube. The light's black wire should hang down the inside.

JOKE BREAK

Why did the gardener plant a light bulb?

To get a power plant!

7 Tape the light's wires to the tube near the bulb on the tube's inside and outside. This tape will keep the light on the edge.

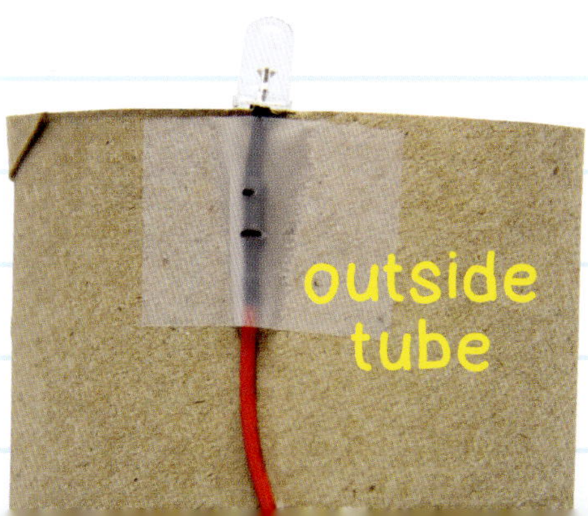

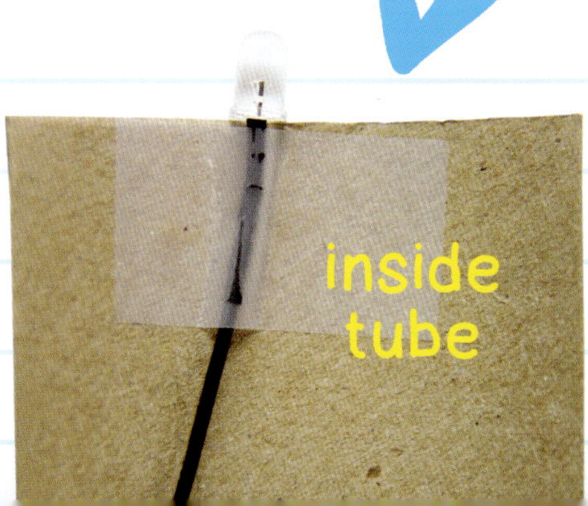

8 Hold the exposed parts of the black wires side by side. Twist the ends together.

9 Bend the twisted wire ends down. Then wrap electrical tape around them.

HINT

If your wires don't reach, shorten the tube. Just remove the battery, and cut off a bit of the tube. Then tape the battery back down. Cut off the same amount on the other tube half.

10 Using clear tape, tape the black wires to the tube.

11 Bring the red wires together on the outside of the tube. Mark where the ends land. It's OK if they don't touch.

12 Place the aluminum tape on the marks.

13 Tape the red wires to the tube. The exposed ends should **hover** above the aluminum tape.

HINT

The aluminum tape makes it easier to complete the **circuit**. The wire ends only need to touch the tape to make the light glow.

HINT

If the light doesn't shine, double check your circuit. Make sure you're pressing both ends to the tape. If it still doesn't work, check the black wires. Did they come disconnected?

14 Using your finger, press both wires against the aluminum tape. The light should turn on.

15 Grab the second half of the tube. Use clear tape to put the halves back together. Your flashlight is complete!

Chapter 3

Get in on the Hi Jinx

The flashlight you made can be used for seeing in the dark. Lights can be used for much more than **illumination**, though! They can be used to create moods and settings. Lighting **technicians** use lights for plays or concerts. A lot of tiny lights can make a stage look like a starry night. Flashing lights can look like lightning. Experiment with your flashlight.

What effects can you make?

Take It One Step More

1. What other material could you use for the flashlight body?

2. Could your flashlight be brighter? Research ways you can make a light brighter.

3. The aluminum tape is a **conductor**. What's the purpose of a conductor in this flashlight?

GLOSSARY

circuit (SUR-kit)—the complete path of an electric current

conductor (kuhn-DUHK-ter)—a material or object that lets electricity or heat move through it

essential (ee-SEN-shuhl)—something that is basic or necessary

exposed (ek-SPOZD)—not covered

hover (HUHV-er)—floating in the air without moving any direction

illumination (ih-loo-muh-NEY-shuhn)—the action of lighting something

responsible (ri-SPON-suh-buhl)—able to be trusted to do what is right or to do things that are expected or required

technician (tek-NISH-uhn)—a person skilled in the details or techniques of a subject, art, or job

LEARN MORE

BOOKS

Gilby, Nancy Benovich, and Katie Gillespie. *First Robotics.* Makerspace. New York: Smartbook Media Inc., 2017.

Greek, Joe. *What Is Electrical Energy?* Forms of Energy. New York: Britannica Educational Publishing in association with Rosen Educational Services, 2018.

Holzweiss, Kristina A. *Amazing Makerspace DIY with Electricity.* A True Book. New York: Children's Press, an imprint of Scholastic Inc., 2018.

WEBSITES

Electricity Science Experiments
www.stevespanglerscience.com/lab/categories/experiments/electricity/

Fun Electricity Facts for Kids
www.sciencekids.co.nz/sciencefacts/electricity.html

Physics for Kids:
Electrical Conductors and Insulators
www.ducksters.com/science/physics/electrical_conductors_and_insulators.php

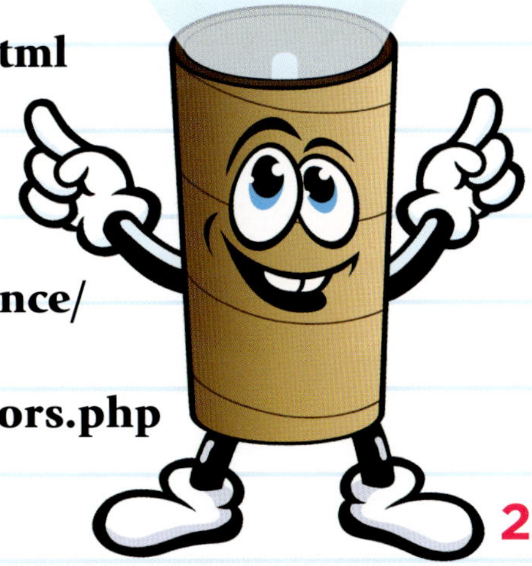

TIPS AND TRICKS

Don't be afraid to ask your adult for help. Some steps can be tricky.

It's OK if your wires' ends aren't exposed. Use a wire stripper to take off as much casing as needed. (Have your adult help with this process.)

You can wrap paper around your finished flashlight to hide the wires. Just tape the paper down. Then mark on the paper where the red wires end beneath it. Pressing on the mark should make the light shine.